MUSIC PAPER

NoteBook

GUITAR CHORD DIAGRAMS

- Larger spaced diagrams
- Vertical/horizontal use
- 8½" x 11" paper
- 100 pages

MUSIC PAPER
NoteBook
GUITAR CHORD DIAGRAMS

by Ashkan Mashhour

ISBN: 978-0-9830498-1-4
Cover & interior design, typography, illustration, prepress: Ashkan Mashhour

Inquiries: ashkan@cheatsheetmusic.com

pelemeleworks.com

Pêle-Mêle WORKS

Possible usage examples:

CHORD DIAGRAMS

VERTICAL USAGE	HORIZONTAL USAGE
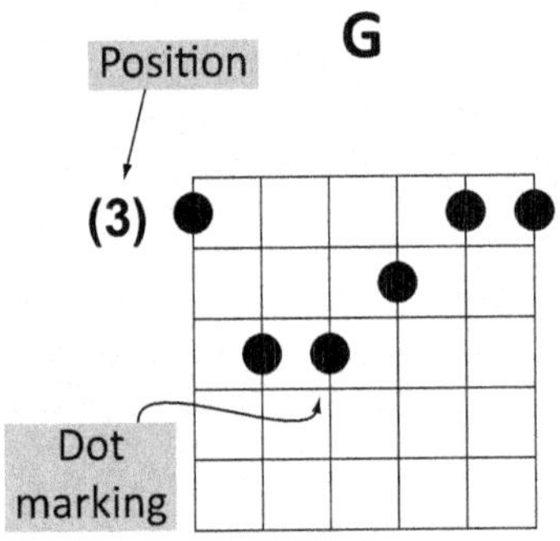	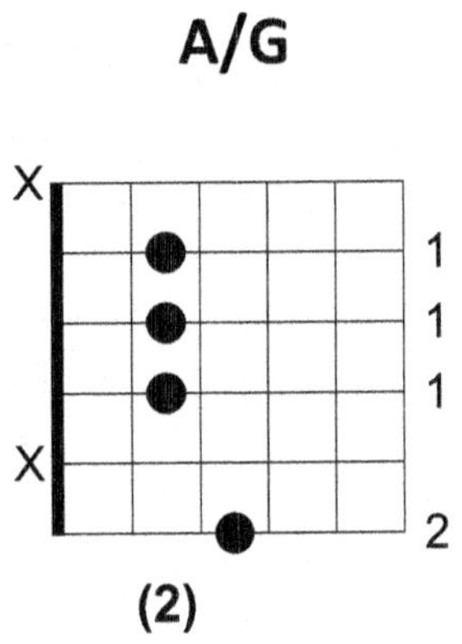
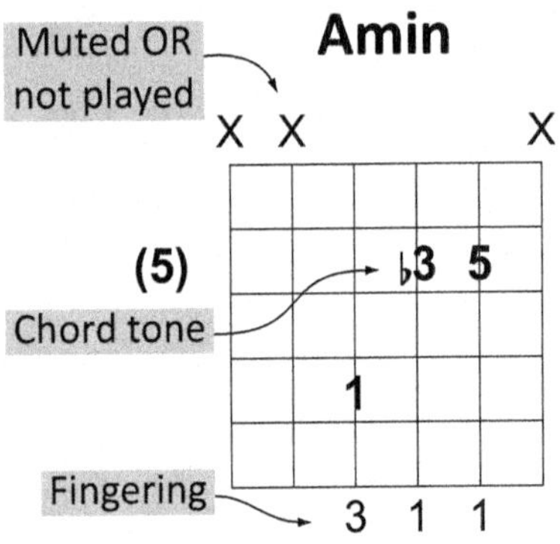	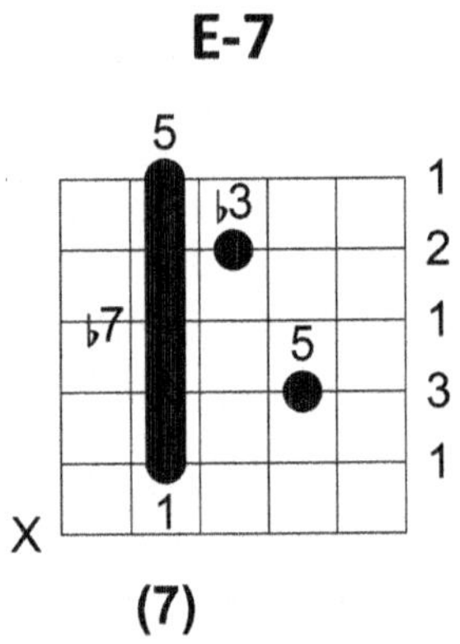
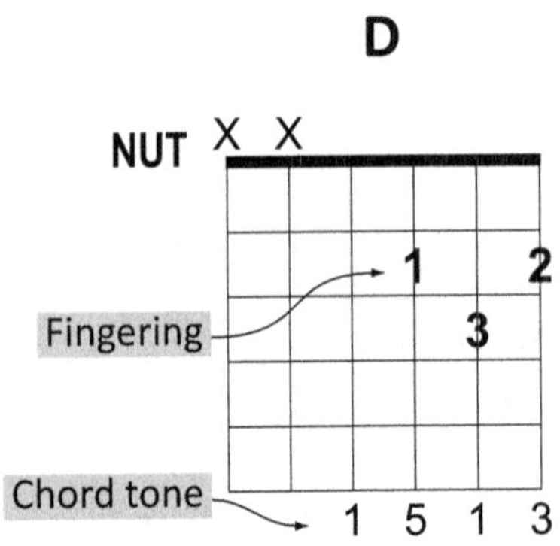	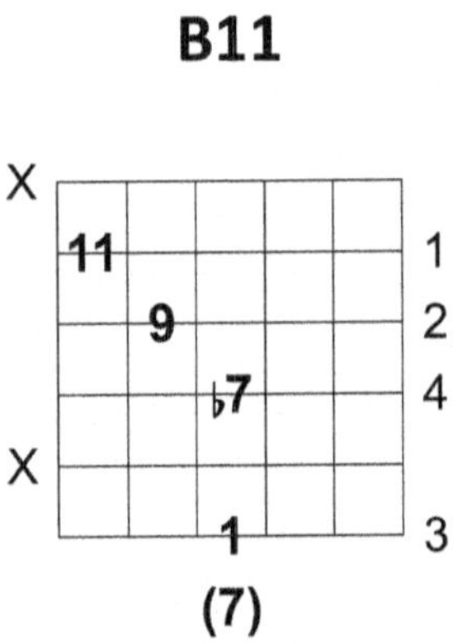

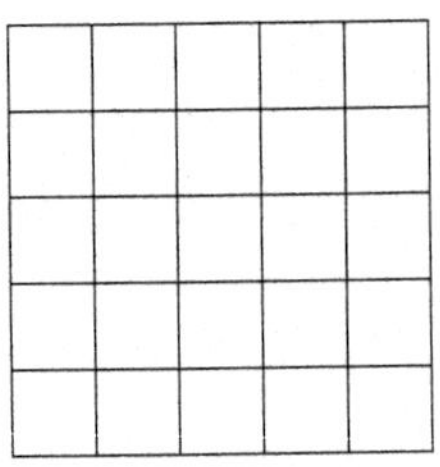
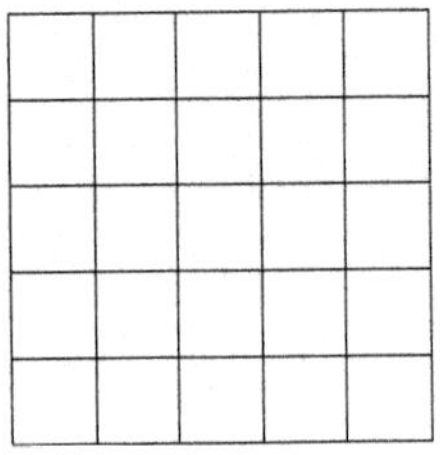
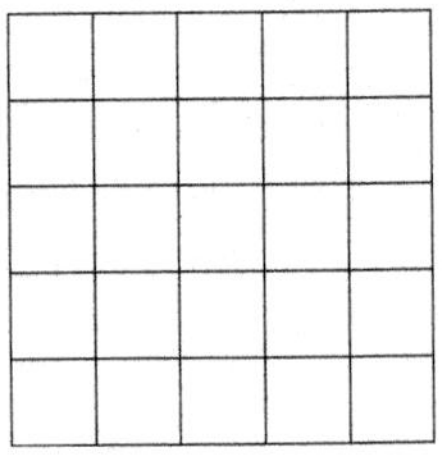
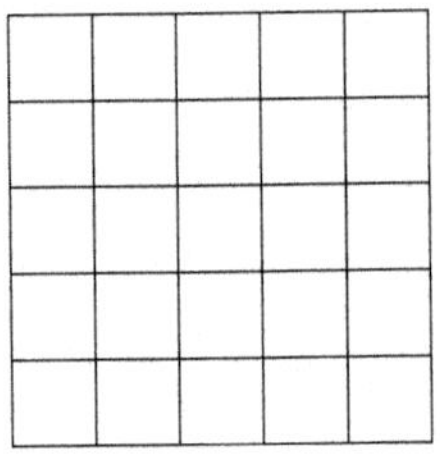
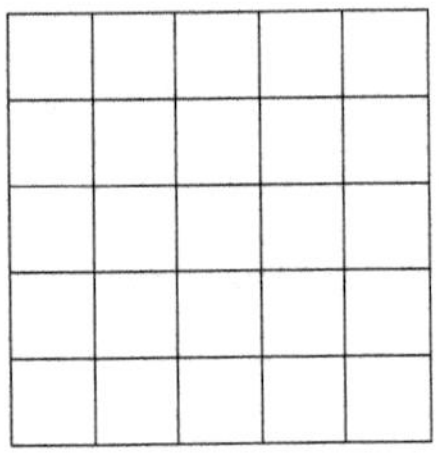
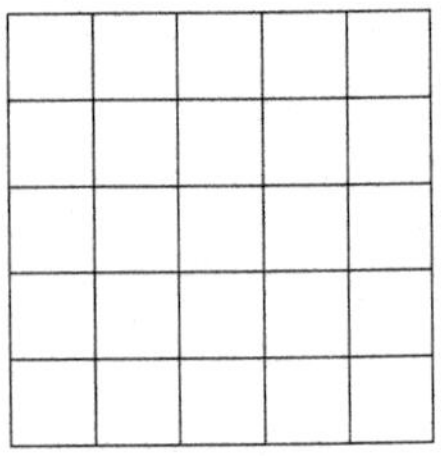
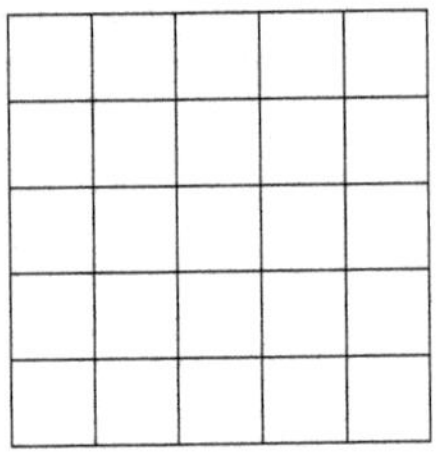
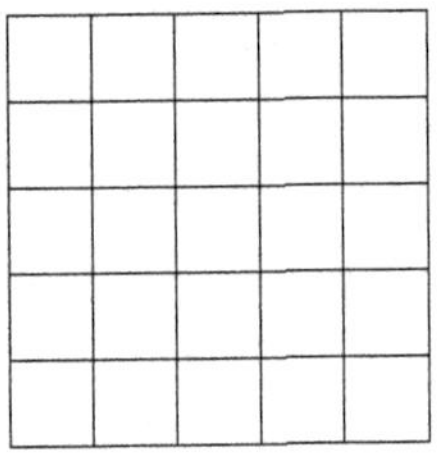
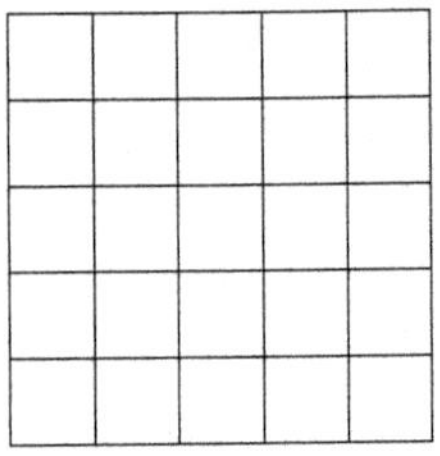
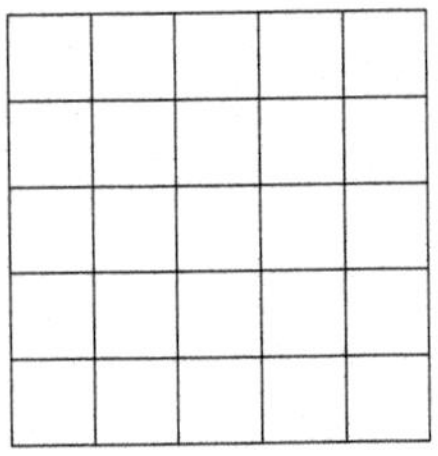
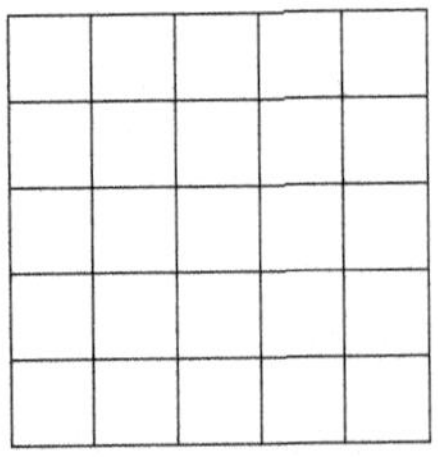
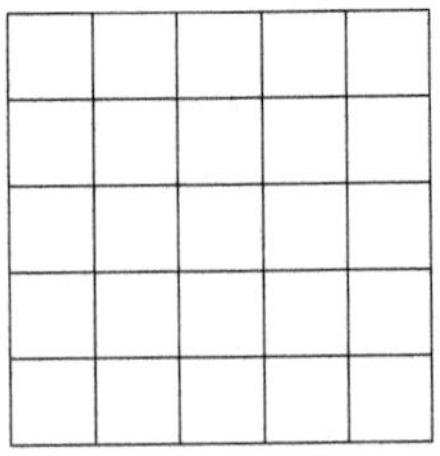
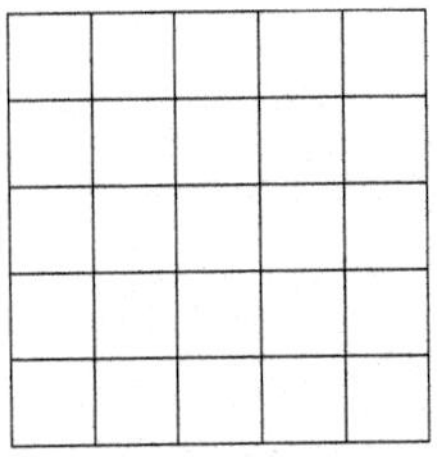
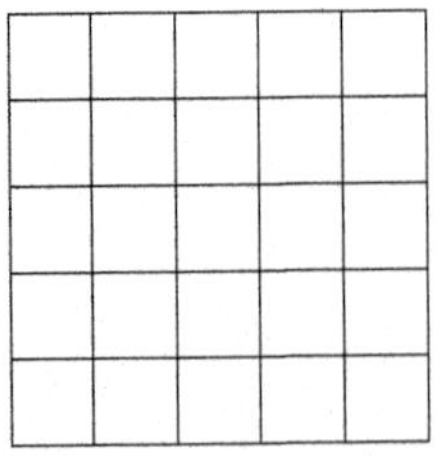
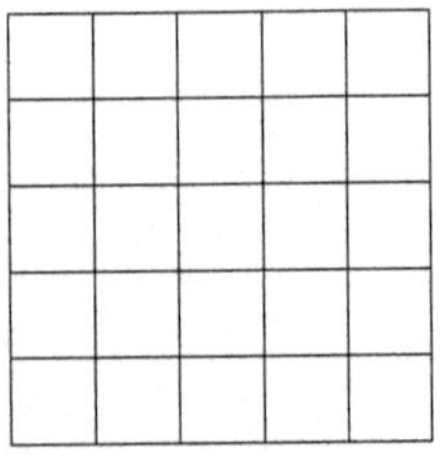

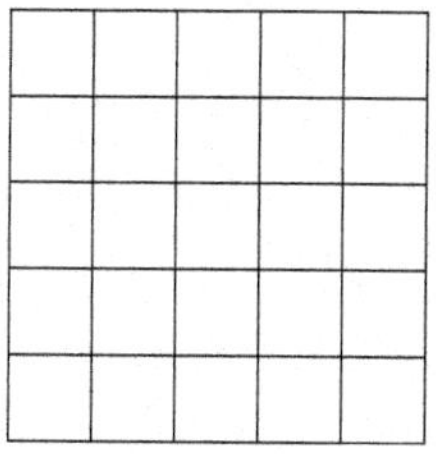
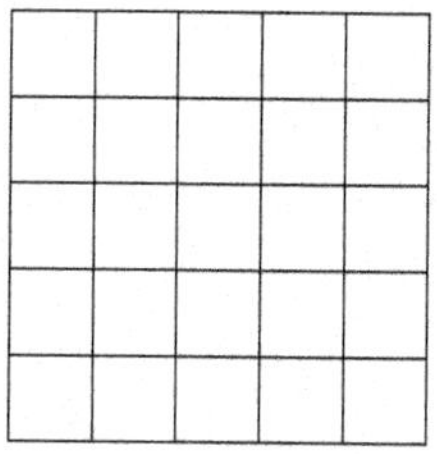
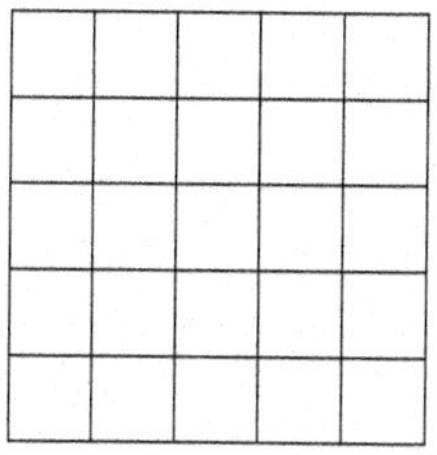
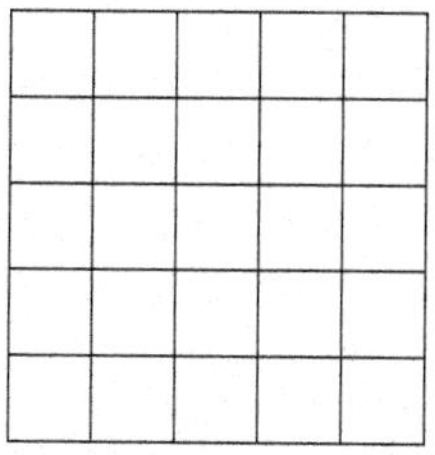
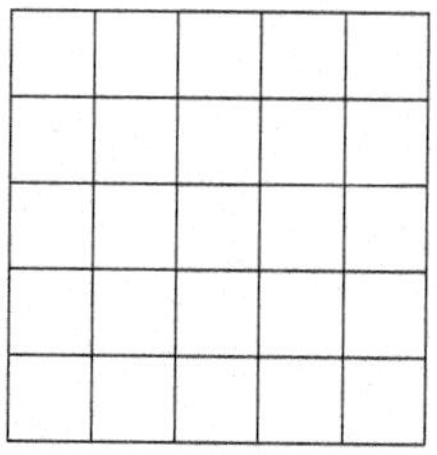
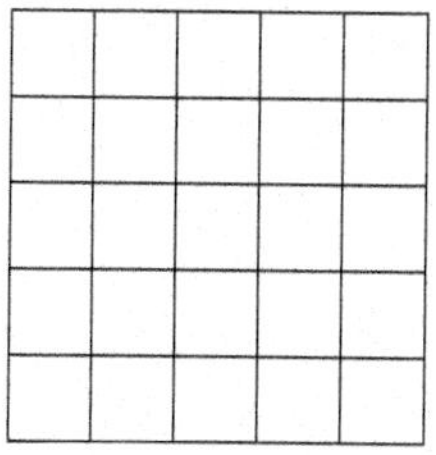
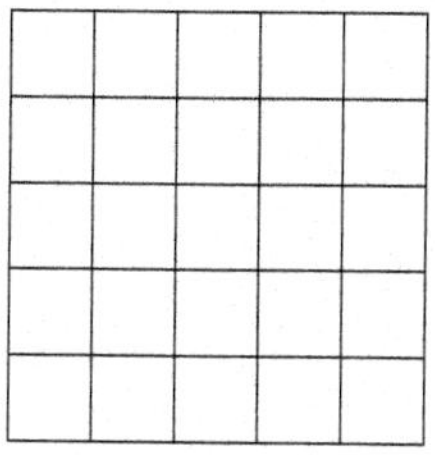
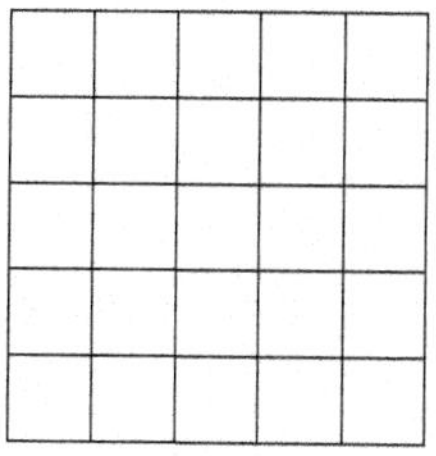
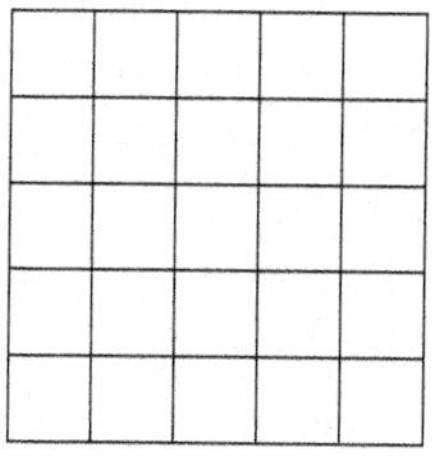
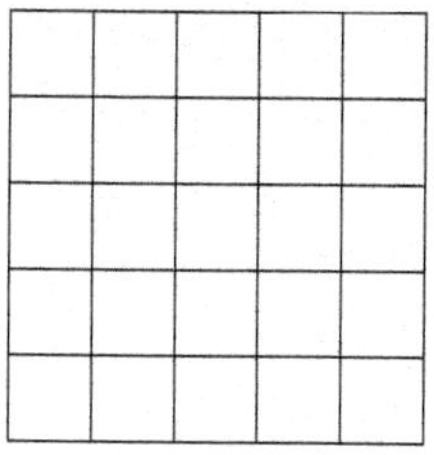
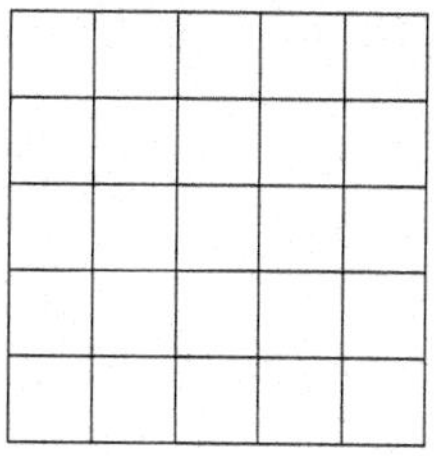
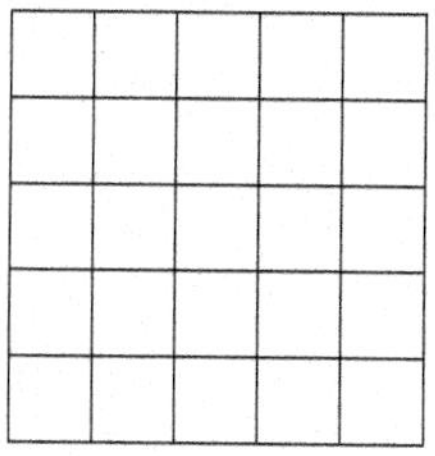
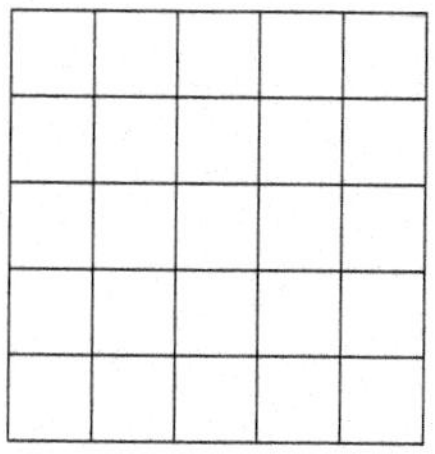
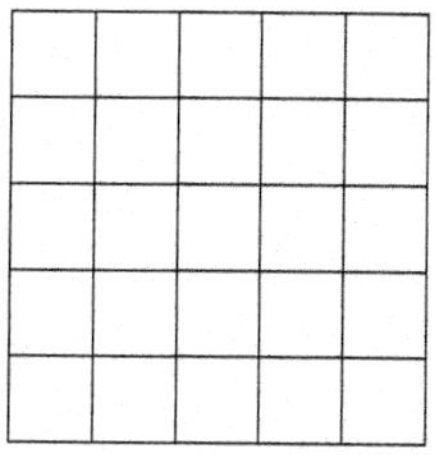
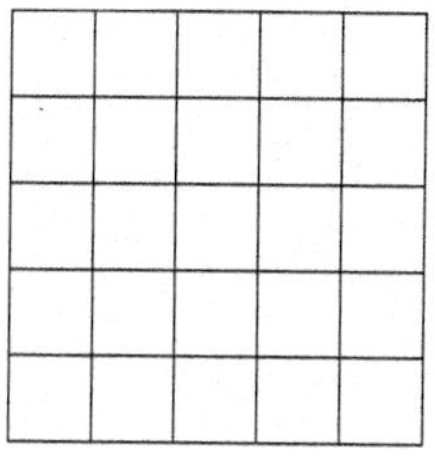

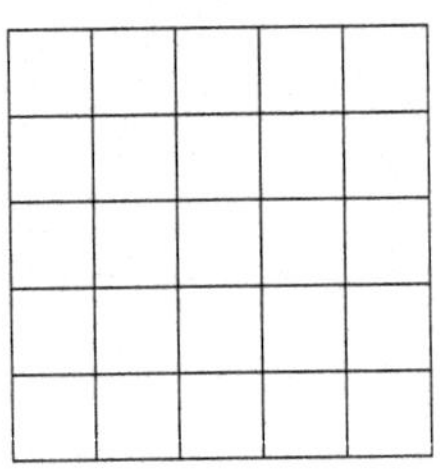
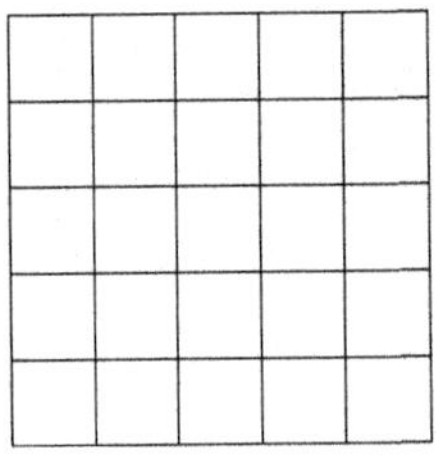
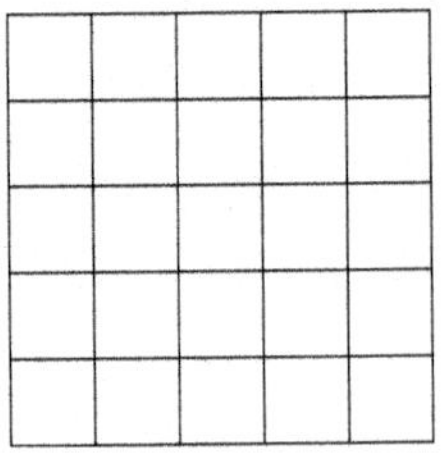
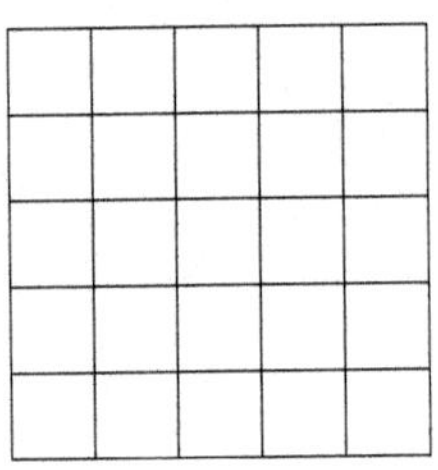
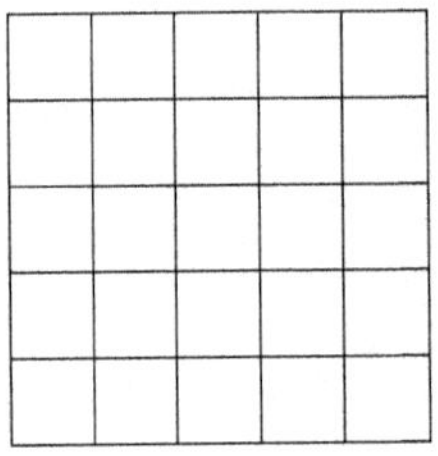
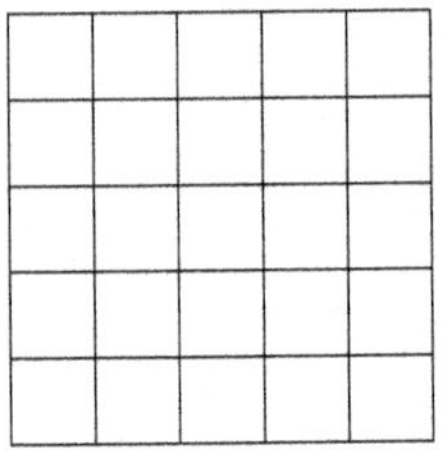
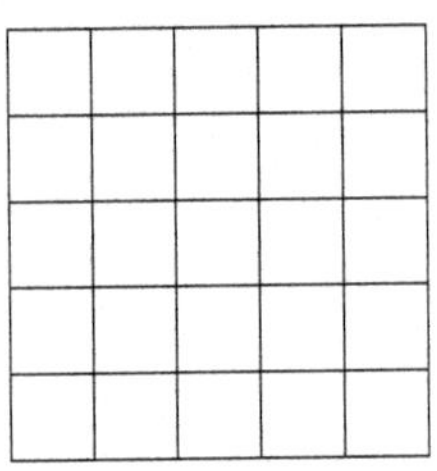
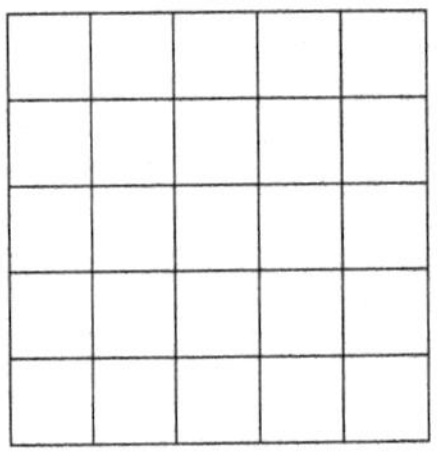
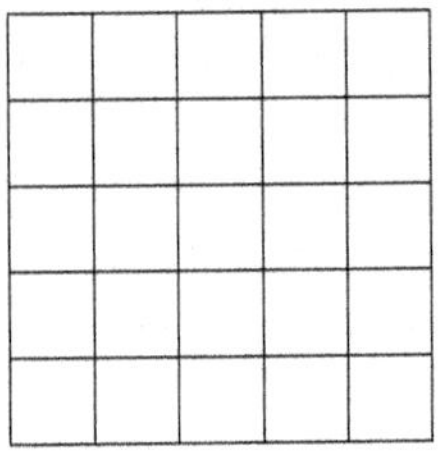
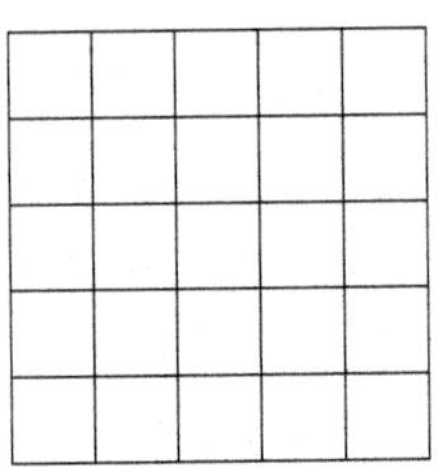
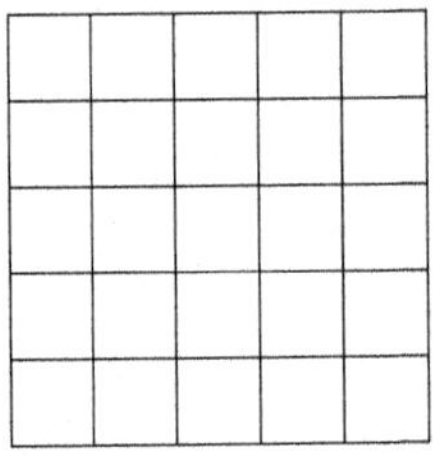
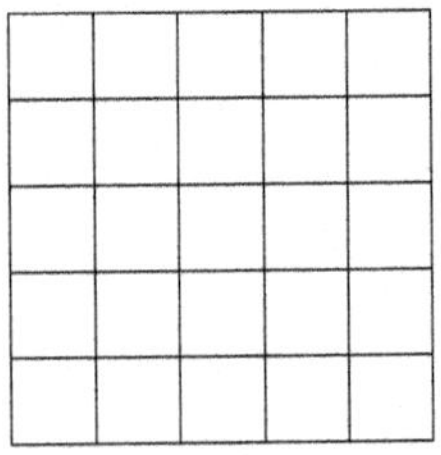
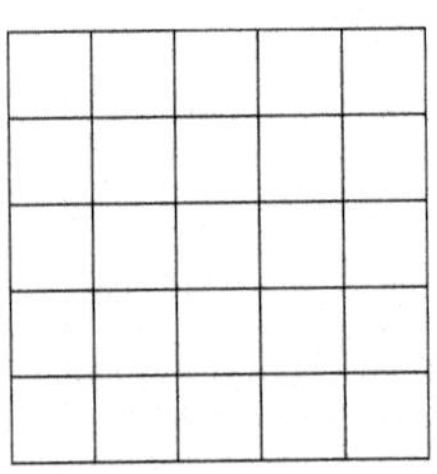
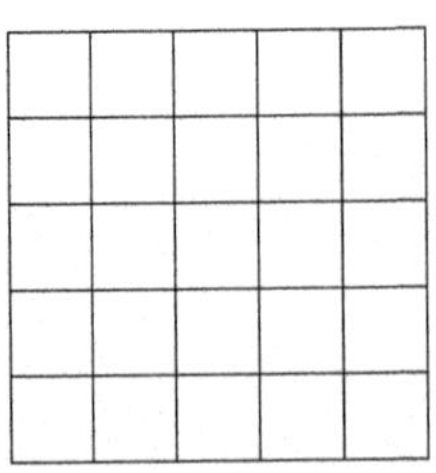
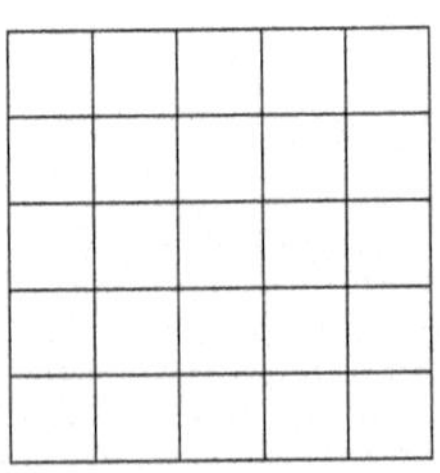

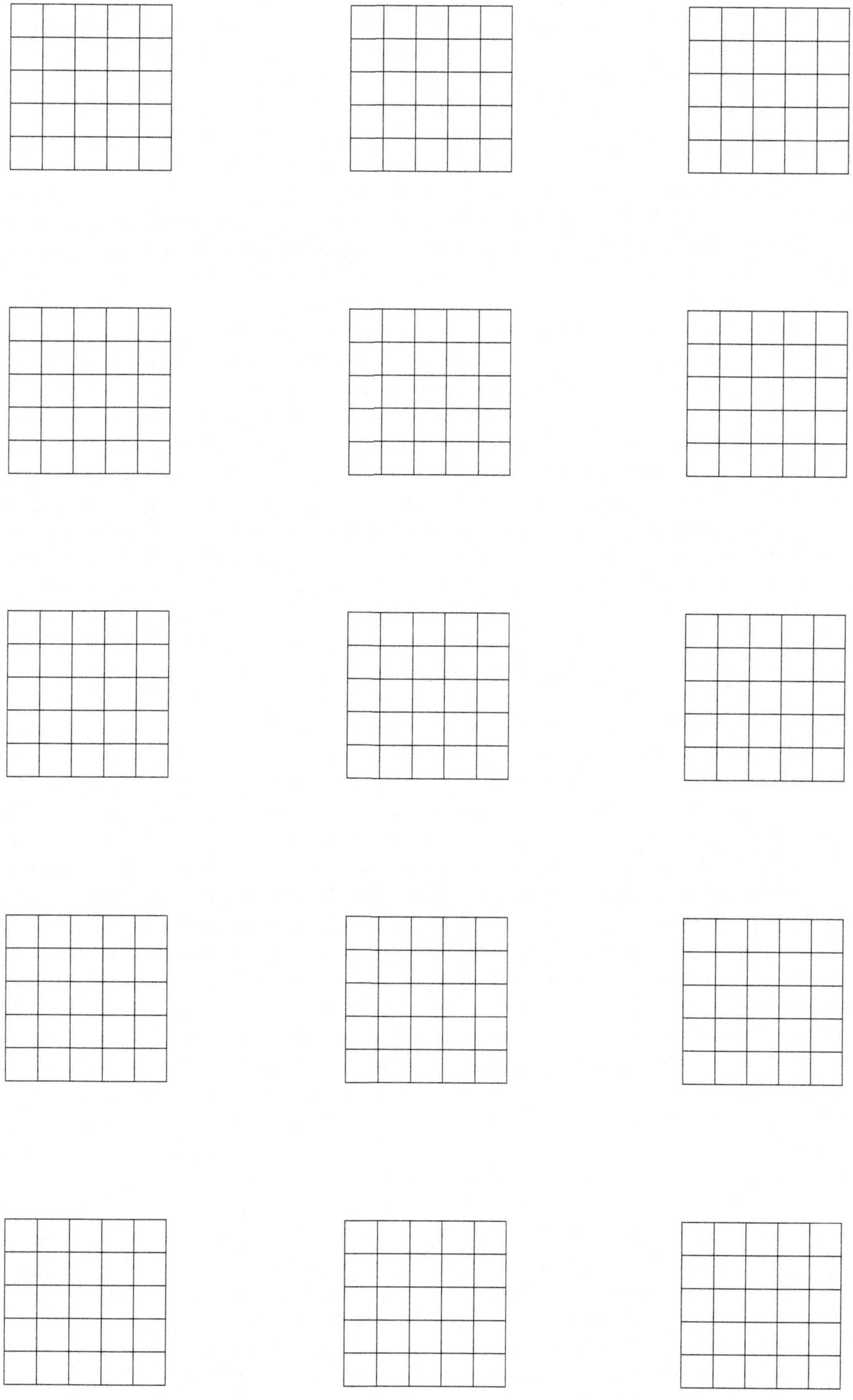

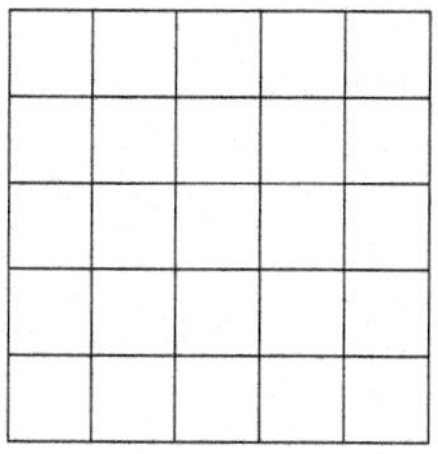
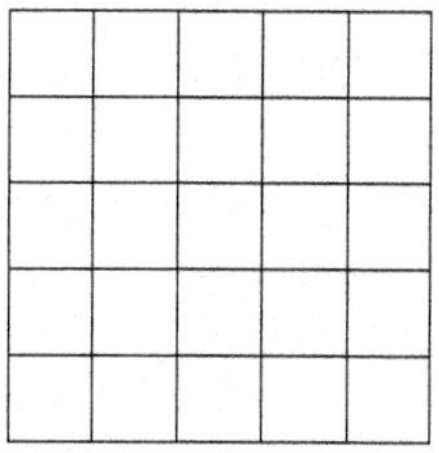
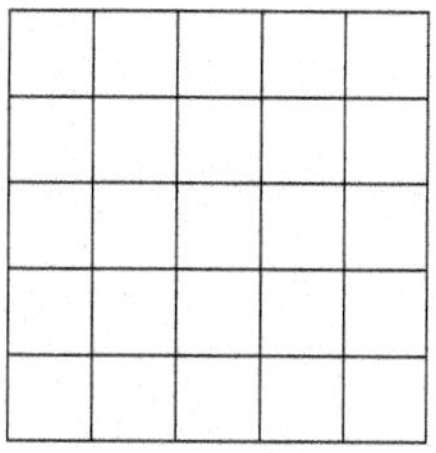
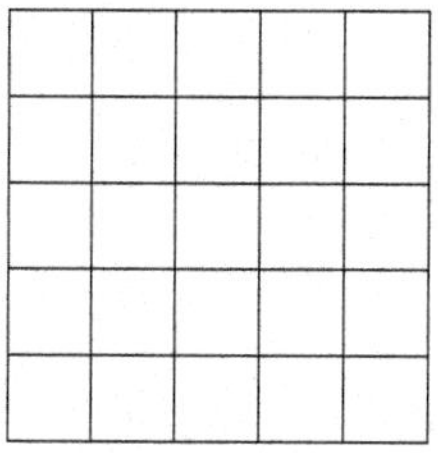
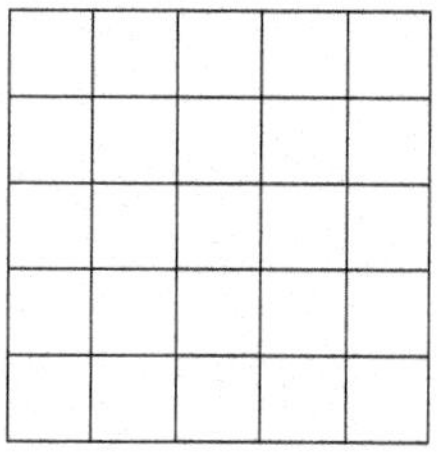
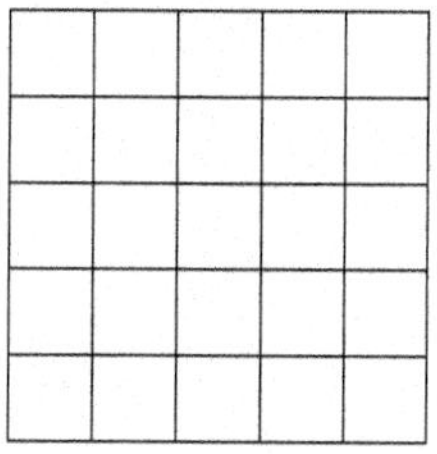
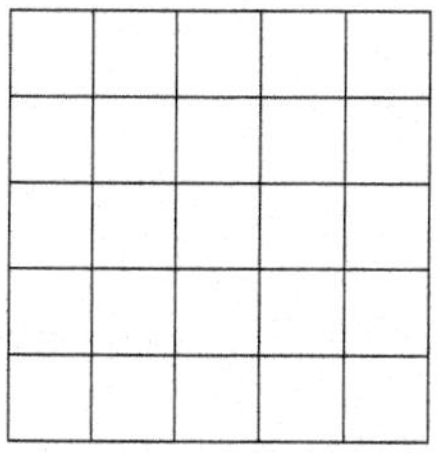
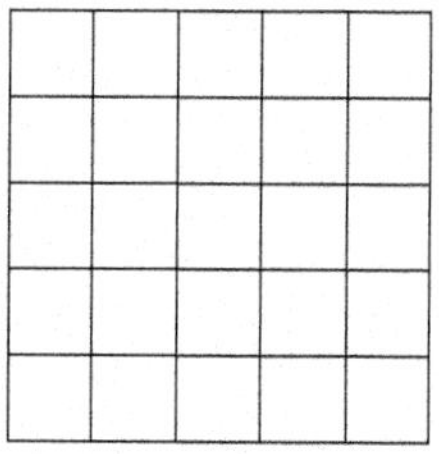
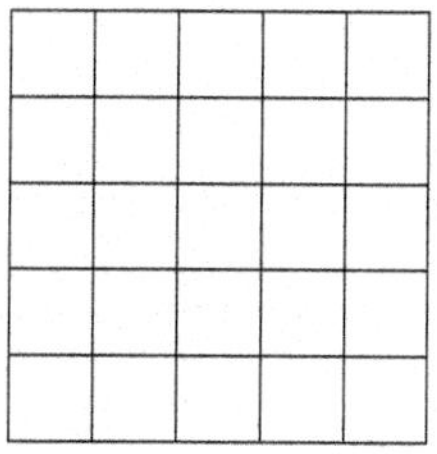
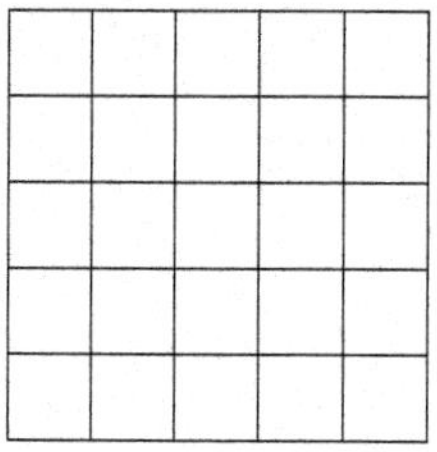
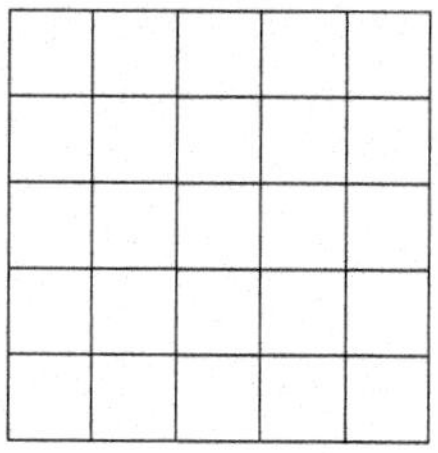
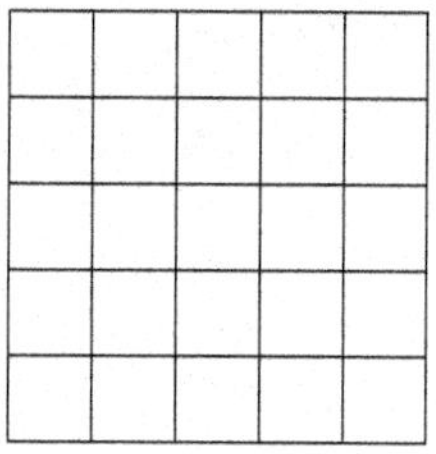
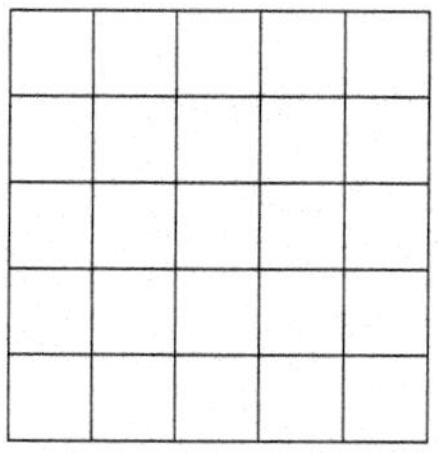
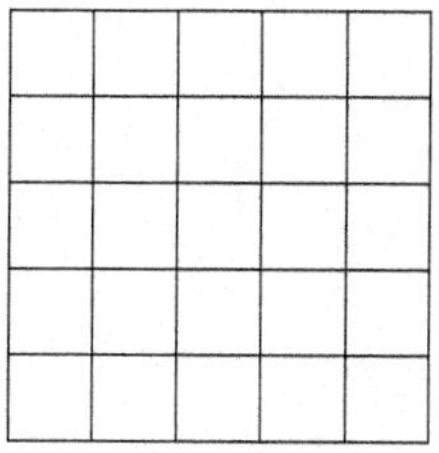
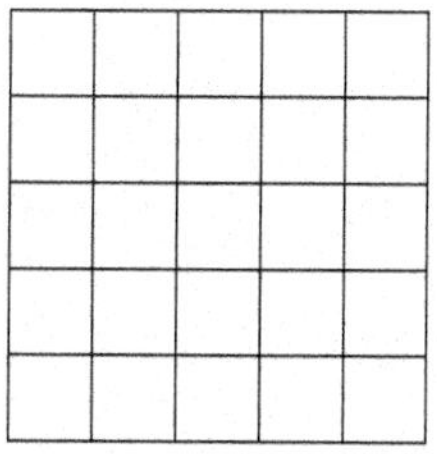

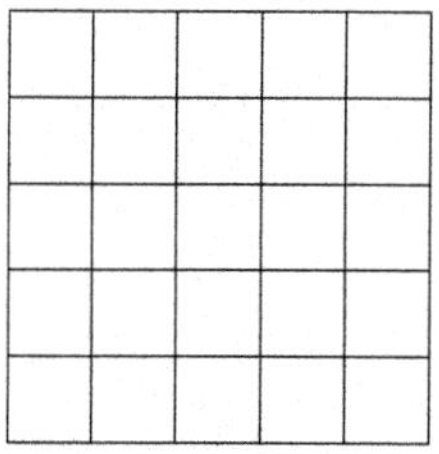
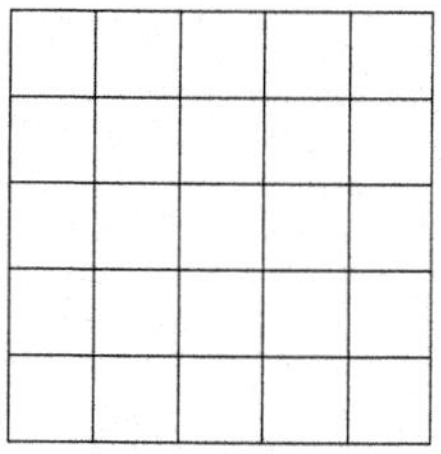
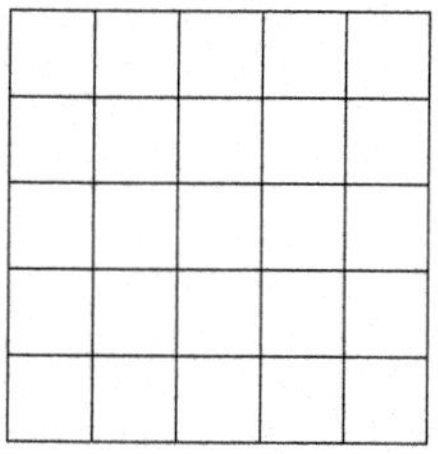
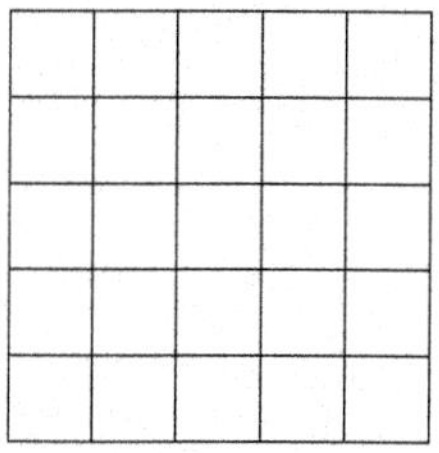
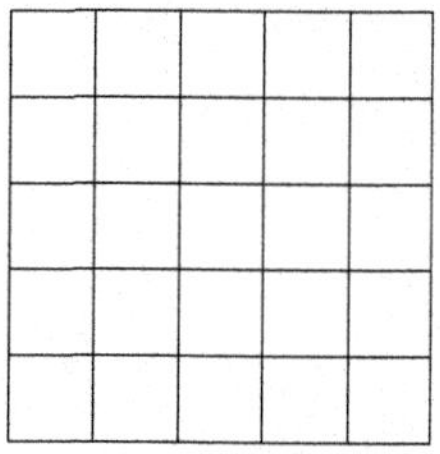
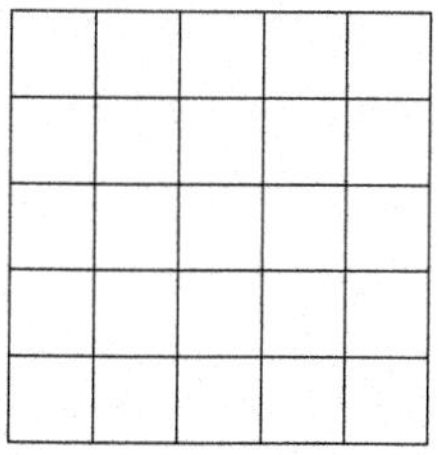
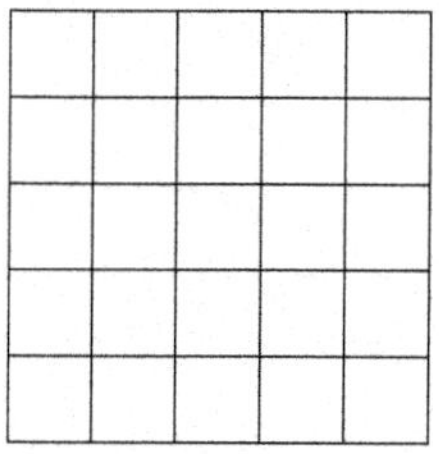
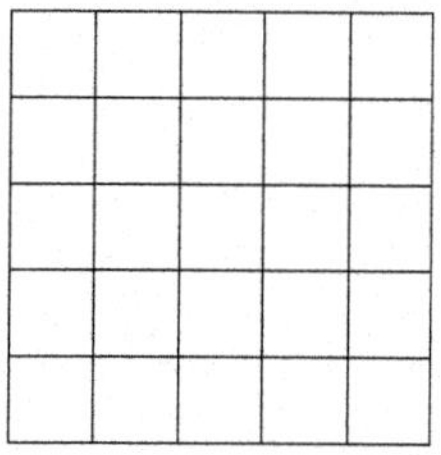
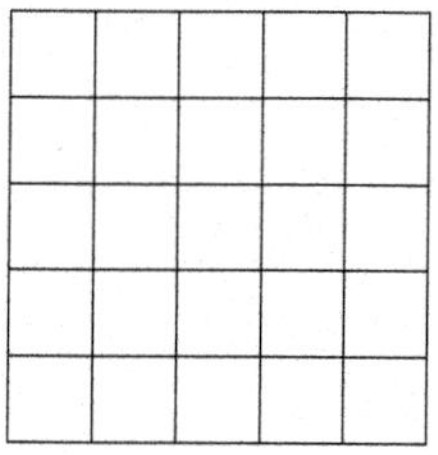
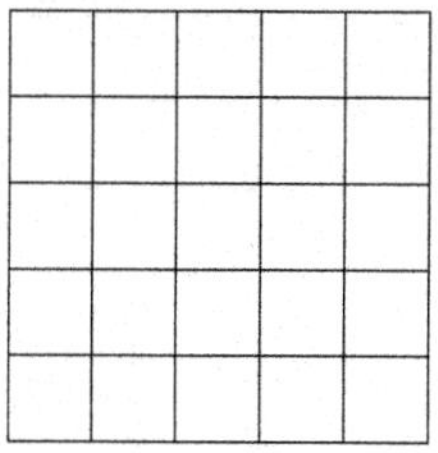
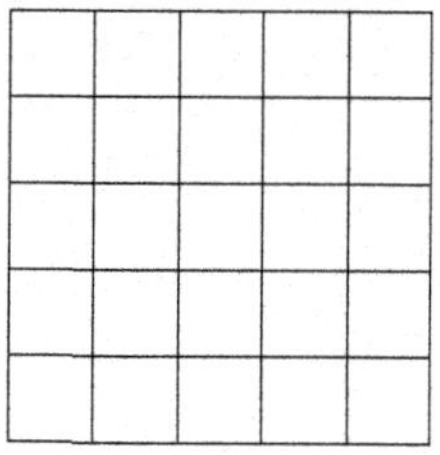
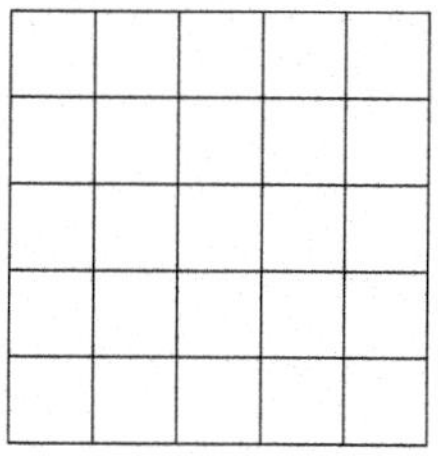
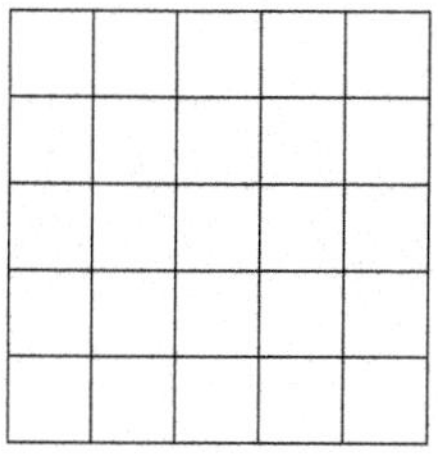
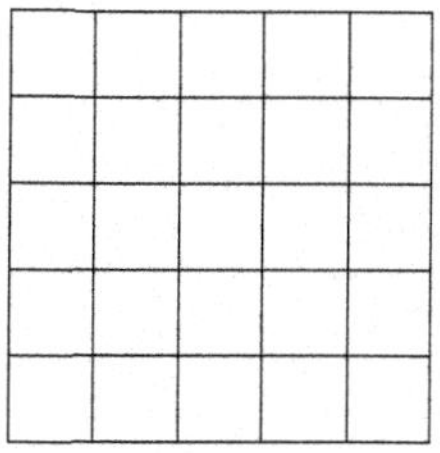
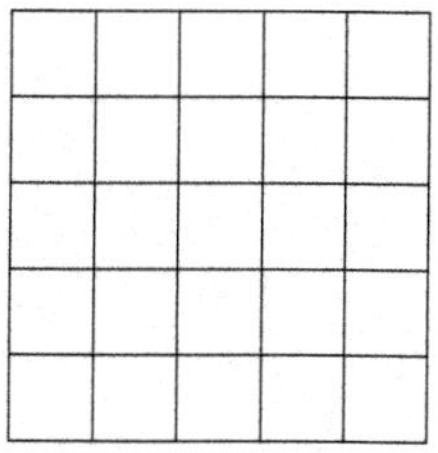

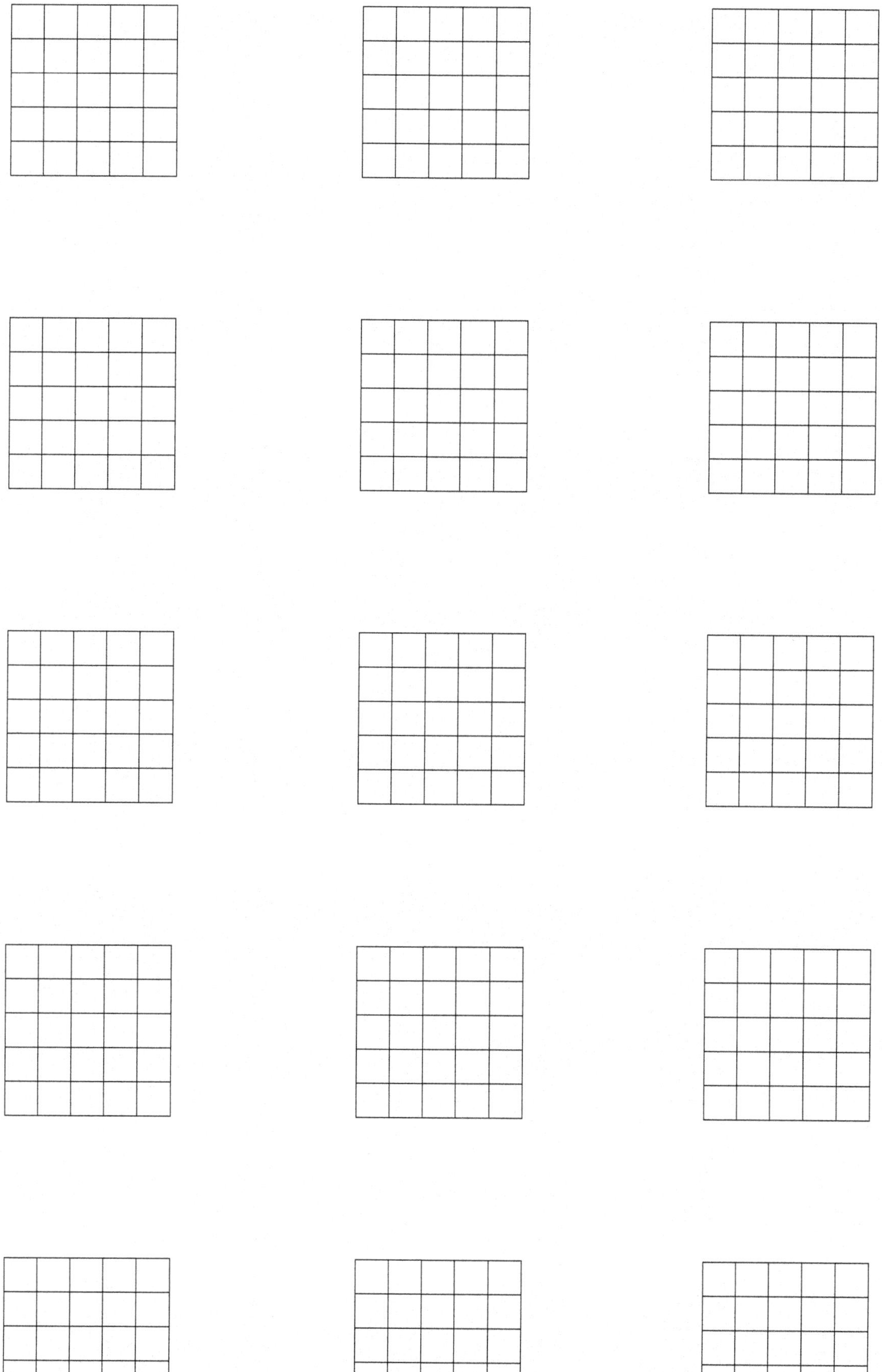

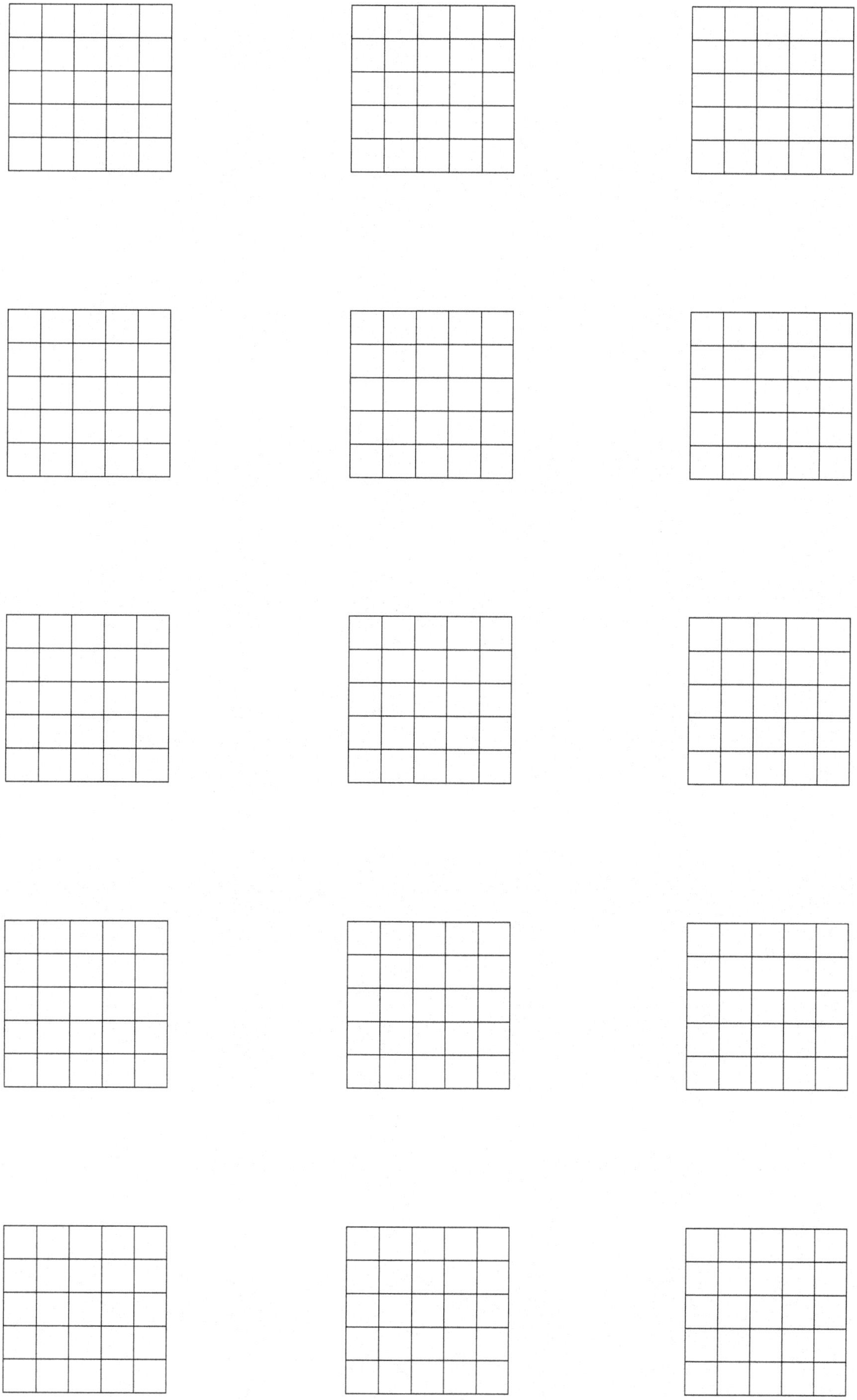

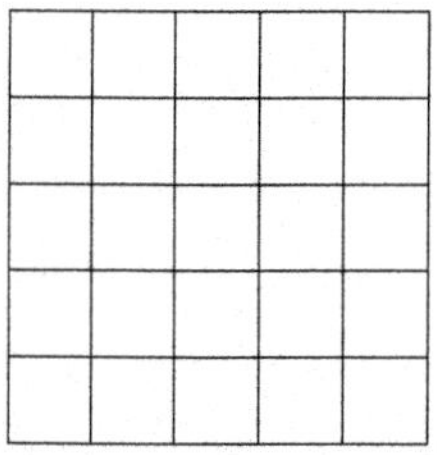
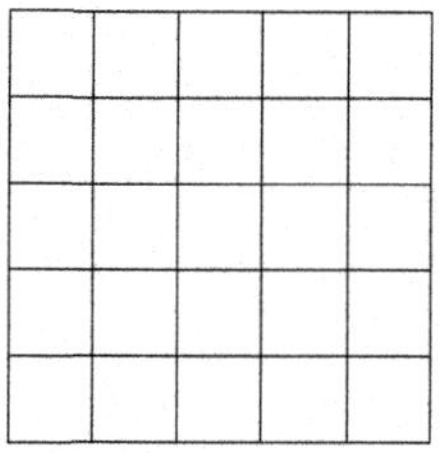
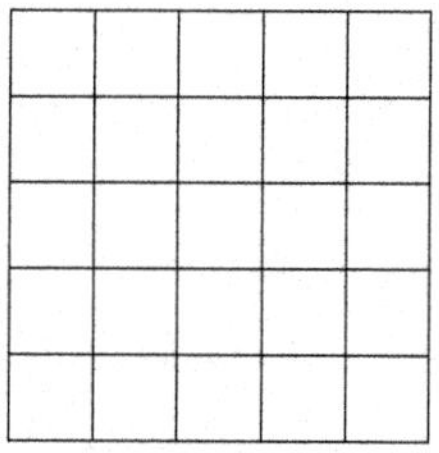
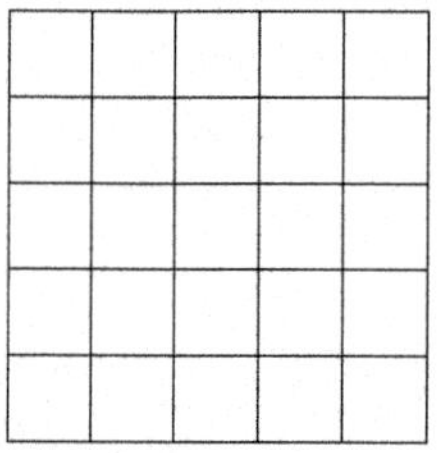
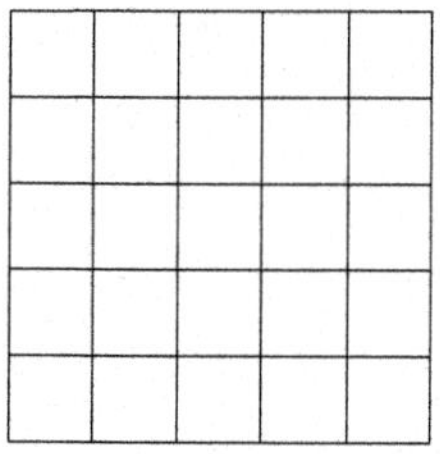
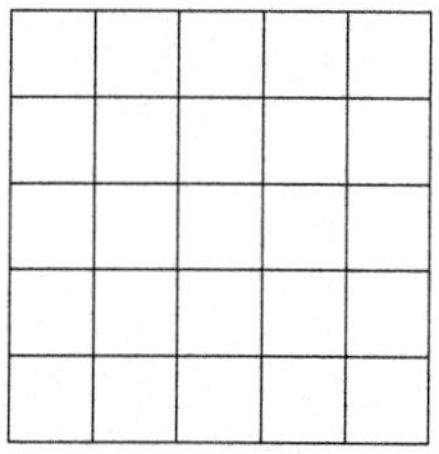
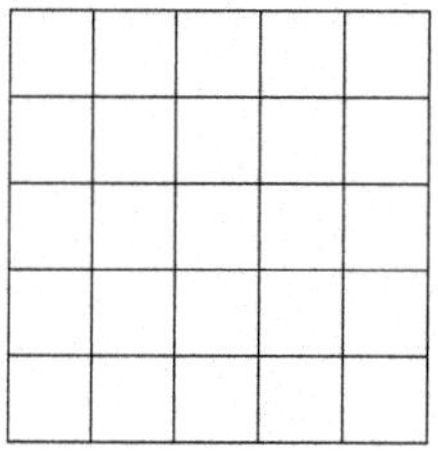
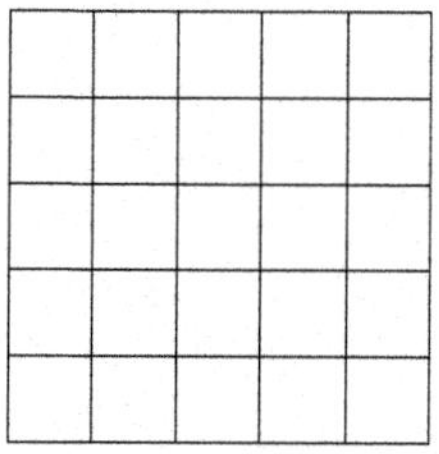
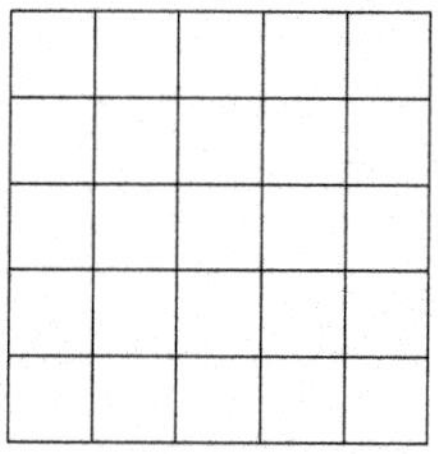
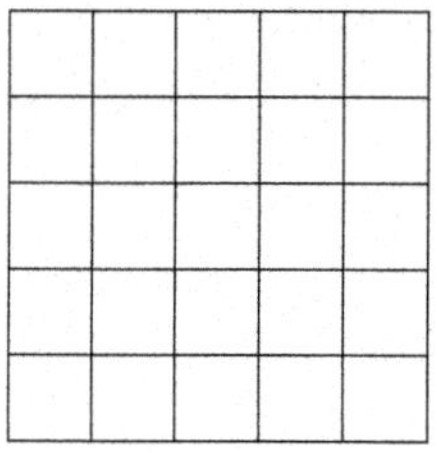
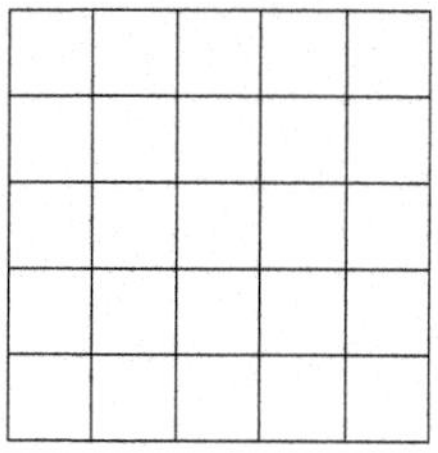
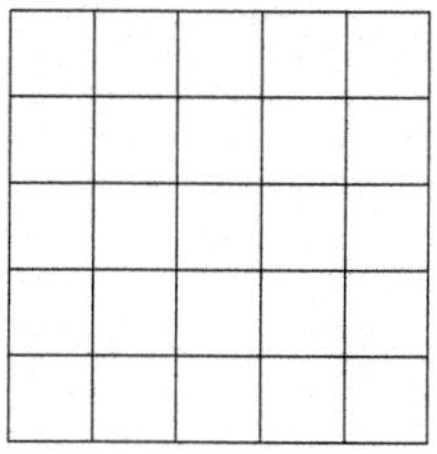
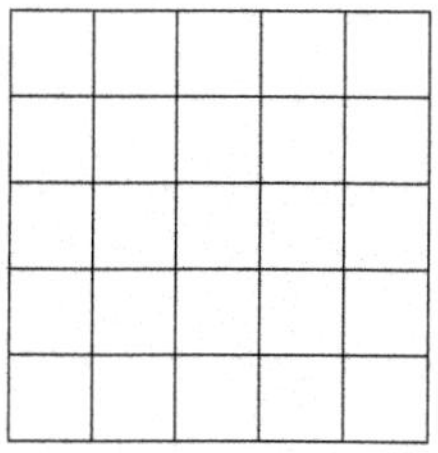
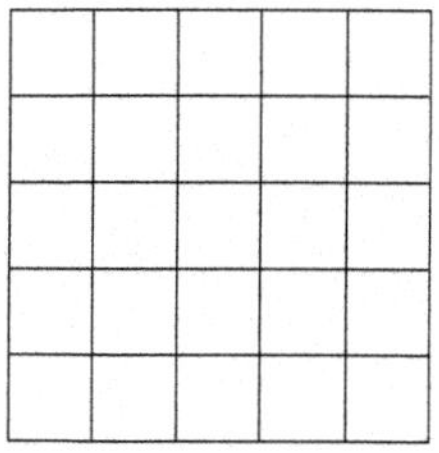
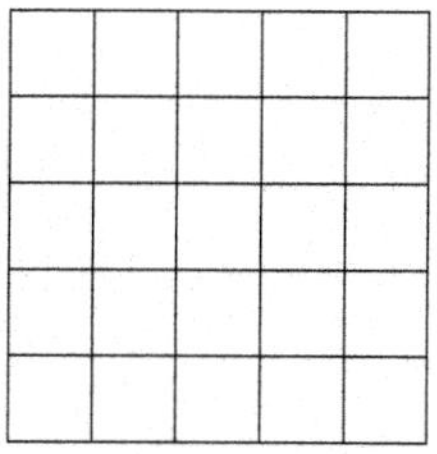

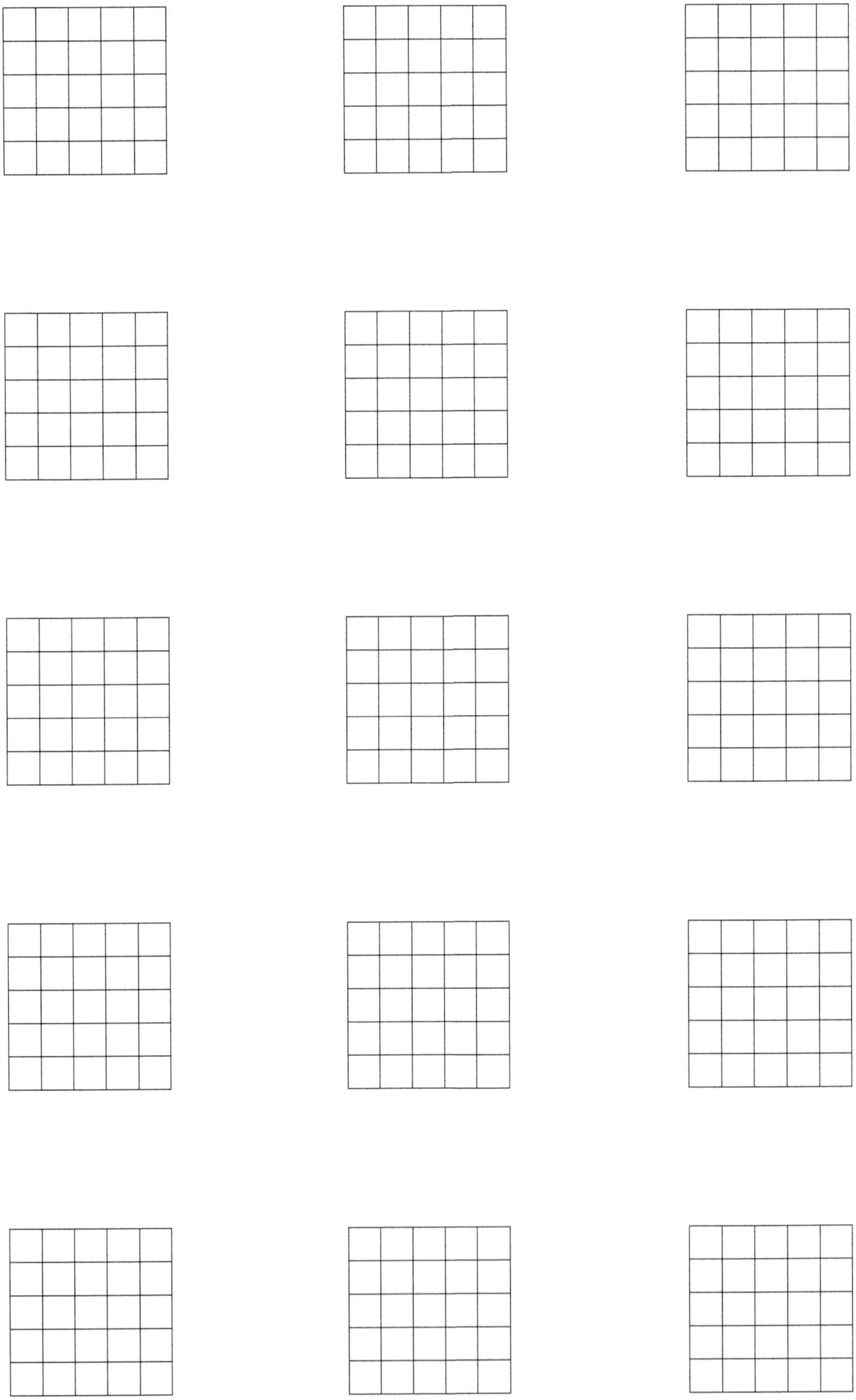

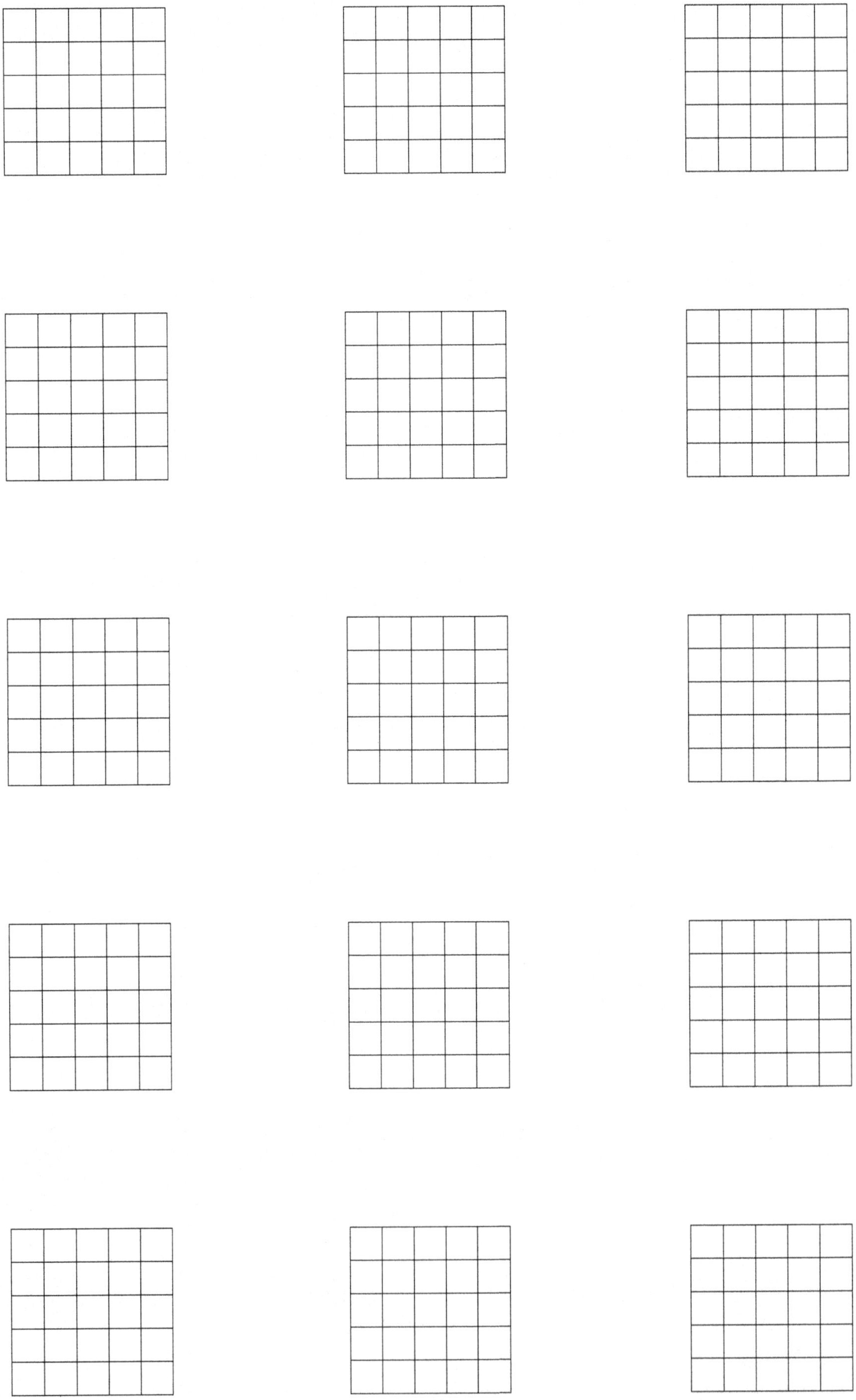

Pêle-Mêle
WORKS

[**pelemeleworks**.com]

- ***MUSIC PAPER*, the manuscript paper series.**
  a range of blank manuscript paper designs for guitar and other instruments, available in pocketbook and notebook formats.
  pelemeleworks.com

- ***CHEATSHEET Music*, the music cheatsheet series.**
  a series of practical cheatsheets on key music topics for the musician, teacher, and student.
  cheatsheetmusic.com

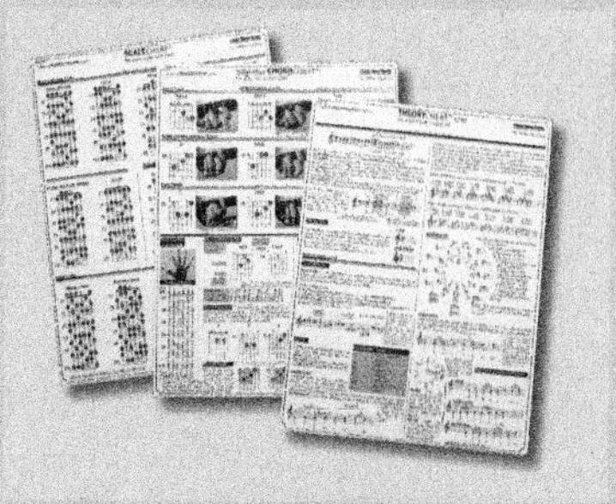

- ***INTERVALLIC FRETBOARD – Towards Improvising on the Guitar.***
  a thought-provoking book on fretboard visualisation, using intervals to understand its geometric properties and navigate its layout.
  intervallicfretboard.com

- ***GUITAR FINGERS – Essential Technique in Pictures.***
  an in-depth tutorial on left hand and right hand technique for guitar, through pictures and short exercises.
  pelemeleworks.com

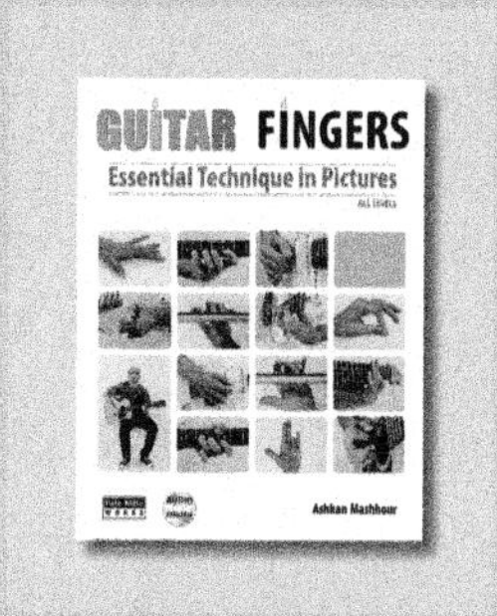

- ***GUITAR NOTE FINDER.***
  a handy aid to help memorise the notes on the fretboard and map them to the music staff.
  pelemeleworks.com

CPSIA information can be obtained
at www.ICGtesting.com
Printed in the USA
BVOW07s1741150218
508111BV00010BA/260/P

9 780983 049814